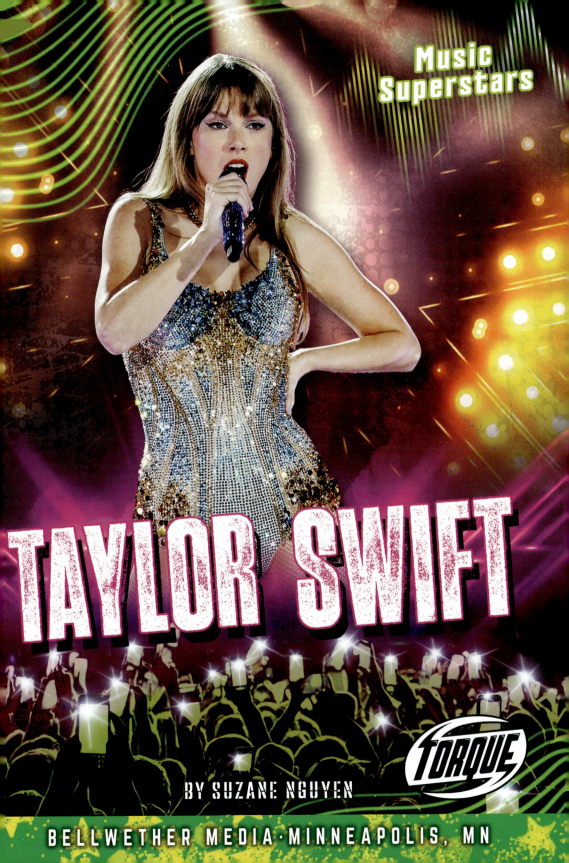

Torque brims with excitement perfect for thrill-seekers of all kinds. Discover daring survival skills, explore uncharted worlds, and marvel at mighty engines and extreme sports. In *Torque* books, anything can happen. Are you ready?

This edition first published in 2025 by Bellwether Media, Inc.

No part of this publication may be reproduced in whole or in part without written permission of the publisher. For information regarding permission, write to Bellwether Media, Inc., Attention: Permissions Department, 6012 Blue Circle Drive, Minnetonka, MN 55343.

Library of Congress Cataloging-in-Publication Data

Names: Nguyen, Suzane, author.
Title: Taylor Swift / by Suzane Nguyen.
Description: Minneapolis, MN : Bellwether Media, 2025. | Series: Music superstars | Includes bibliographical references and index. | Audience: Ages 7-12 | Audience: Grades 4-6 | Summary: "Engaging images accompany information about Taylor Swift. The combination of high-interest subject matter and light text is intended for students in grades 3 through 7"– Provided by publisher.
Identifiers: LCCN 2024046996 (print) | LCCN 2024046997 (ebook) | ISBN 9798893042672 (library binding) | ISBN 9798893043648 (ebook)
Subjects: LCSH: Swift, Taylor, 1989–Juvenile literature. | Singers–United States–Biography–Juvenile literature. | Country musicians–United States–Biography–Juvenile literature. | LCGFT: Biographies.
Classification: LCC ML3930.S989 N53 2025 (print) | LCC ML3930.S989 (ebook) | DDC 782.42164092 [B]–dc23/eng/20241008
LC record available at https://lccn.loc.gov/2024046996
LC ebook record available at https://lccn.loc.gov/2024046997

Text copyright © 2025 by Bellwether Media, Inc. TORQUE and associated logos are trademarks and/or registered trademarks of Bellwether Media, Inc.

Editor: Rachael Barnes   Designer: Josh Brink

Printed in the United States of America, North Mankato, MN.

TABLE OF CONTENTS

A Mega Tour	4
Who Is Taylor Swift?	6
Getting Into Music	8
Rising to Fame	12
For the Fans	20
Glossary	22
To Learn More	23
Index	24

A MEGA TOUR

The stage lights up! Taylor Swift and her band play the first notes of her song "Fearless." Taylor plays the guitar as she walks to the microphone to sing.

2024 ERAS TOUR

RECORD BREAKER

The Eras Tour holds the record for highest-earning music tour ever!

Partway through the song, Taylor lifts her hands up to make a heart. Thousands of fans do it, too. It is a great night at the 2024 Eras Tour!

WHO IS TAYLOR SWIFT?

Taylor Swift is a singer and songwriter. She also plays many instruments. Taylor is one of the biggest pop stars in the world. She holds the **solo** artist record for most weeks on top of the *Billboard* charts!

TAYLOR SWIFT

Birthday
December 13, 1989

Hometown
West Reading, Pennsylvania

Types of Music
pop, country, folk

First Hit
"Tim McGraw"

Taylor supports many **charities**, including animal shelters and **food banks**. She has also given money to help people after **natural disasters**.

7

GETTING INTO MUSIC

Taylor became interested in music at a young age. Her grandma was an opera singer. She **inspired** Taylor. At age 10, Taylor started to sing at small events.

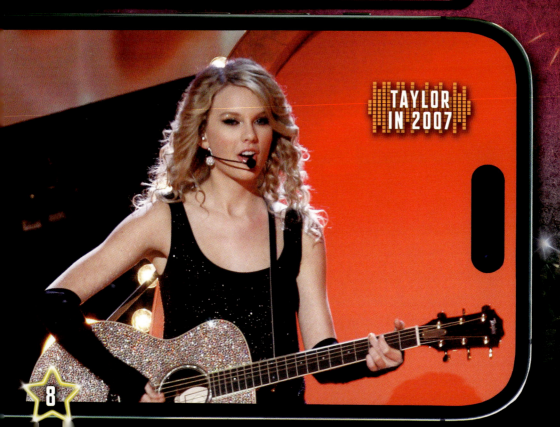

TAYLOR IN 2007

FAVORITES

Lucky Number
13

Coffee
caramel nonfat latte

Movie
Love Actually

Pet
cats

When Taylor was 11, she sang "The Star-Spangled Banner" at a basketball game. Taylor began to write her own songs at age 12. She learned to play the guitar, too!

Taylor's parents moved their family to Tennessee to support her music dreams. At age 14, Taylor signed a **contract** with what is now Sony Music Publishing.

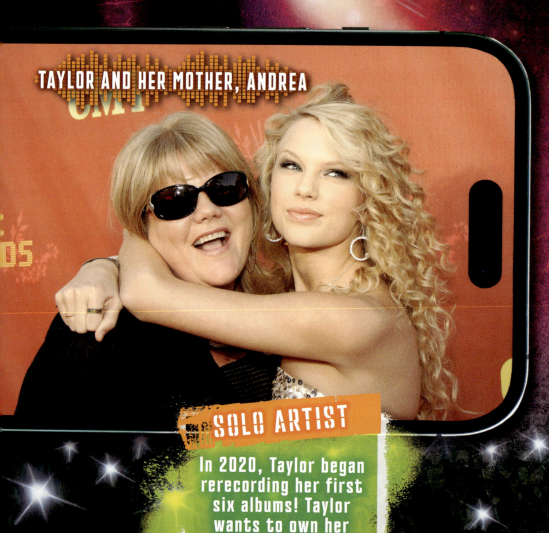

TAYLOR AND HER MOTHER, ANDREA

SOLO ARTIST

In 2020, Taylor began rerecording her first six albums! Taylor wants to own her music and control how it is used.

Taylor started performing many of her own songs. She was noticed by a new **record label** called Big Machine. Taylor signed a contract with them in 2006.

RISING TO FAME

In 2006, Taylor **released** her first song, "Tim McGraw." The country song made it onto the *Billboard* Hot 100 chart. That same year her first album, *Taylor Swift*, came out.

Taylor's talent was recognized at the 2007 **CMA Awards**. She won an award for best new artist of the year! More people started listening to her music.

TIMELINE

– 2006 –
Taylor releases her first album, *Taylor Swift*

– 2010 –
Taylor wins four Grammys for the album *Fearless* and the song "White Horse"

2007 CMA AWARDS

— 2014 —
Taylor releases her album *1989*

— 2020 —
Taylor releases two albums, *Folklore* and *Evermore*

— 2024 —
Taylor's album *Midnights* wins two Grammys

Taylor released her second album, *Fearless*, in 2008. It quickly became number one on the *Billboard* charts. Her song "Love Story" was a fan favorite and helped her album sell well.

2008 PERFORMANCE OF "LOVE STORY"

AWARDS

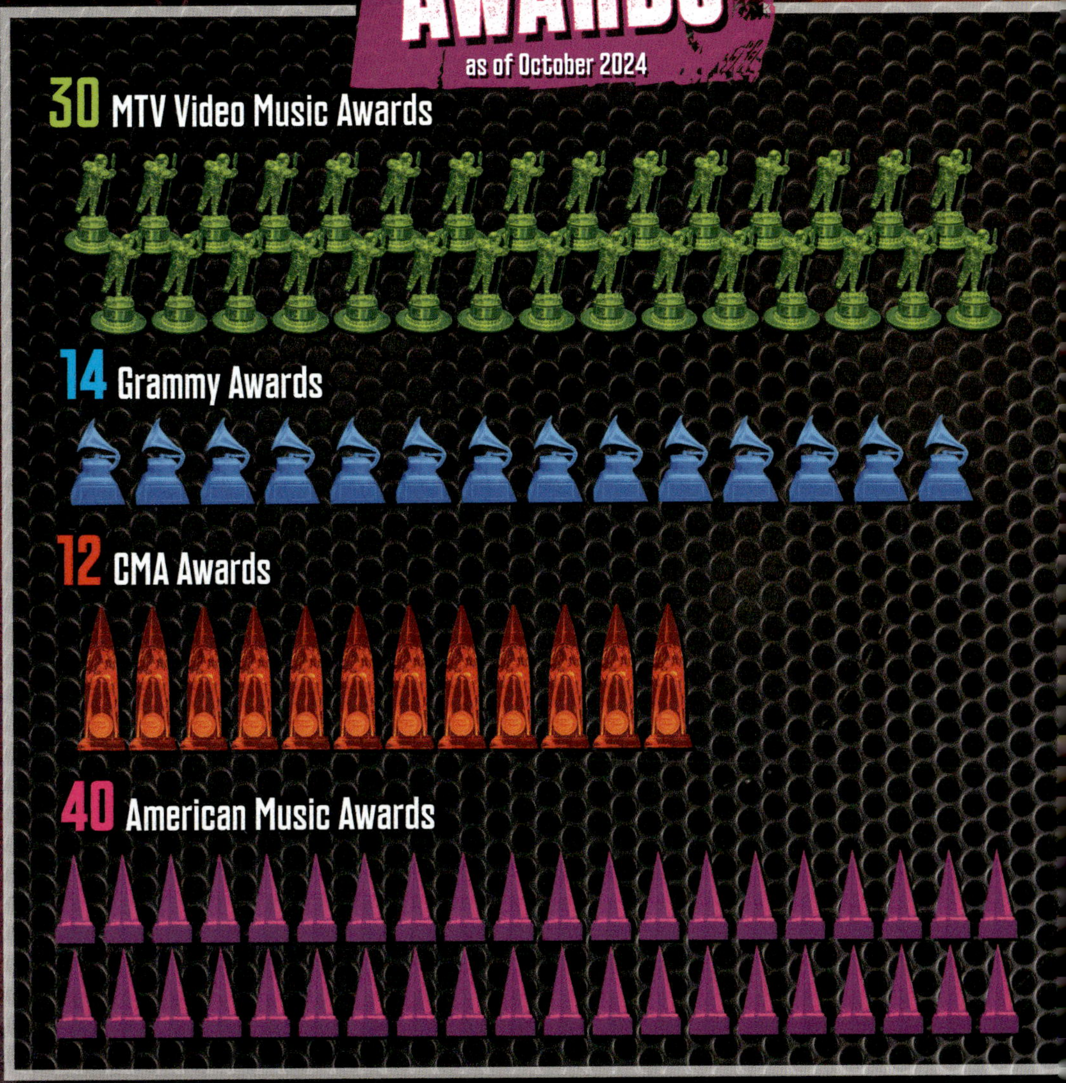

as of October 2024

30 MTV Video Music Awards

14 Grammy Awards

12 CMA Awards

40 American Music Awards

Taylor won four **Grammy Awards** in 2010. The next year, the CMA Awards named her 2011's Entertainer of the Year!

15

Taylor's album *Red* came out in 2012. The song "We Are Never Ever Getting Back Together" made it onto the *Billboard* Hot 100 chart. In its second week, it hit the top spot and stayed there for three weeks!

STAR BAKER

One of Taylor's favorite things to do is bake. Her chai sugar cookies are famous!

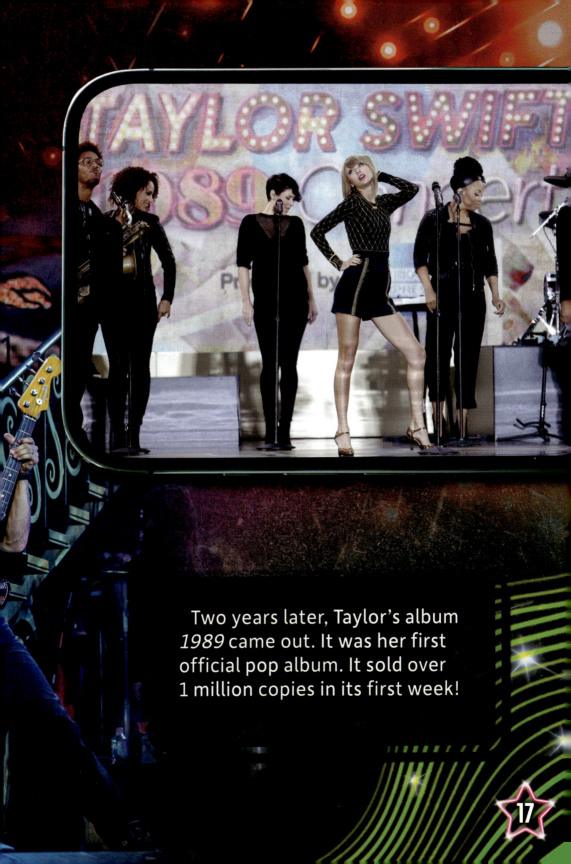

Two years later, Taylor's album *1989* came out. It was her first official pop album. It sold over 1 million copies in its first week!

Taylor released her *Midnights* album in 2022. The album later won two Grammys. In March 2023, Taylor started traveling the world for her Eras Tour. The show is over three hours long!

Taylor's album *The Tortured Poets Department* came out in 2024. Millions of people listened to it in a single day!

FOR THE FANS

Taylor Swift fans are called Swifties. They have listening parties for Taylor's new albums. Taylor's songs talk about love and her personal life. Many fans think her music is catchy and **relatable**.

WOMAN OF THE YEAR

Taylor won the *Billboard* Woman of the Year award in 2011 and 2014. She is the only artist to win the award twice!

PLAYLIST

"Teardrops On My Guitar" (2006)

"We Are Never Ever Getting Back Together" (2012)

"Shake It Off" (2014)

"Cruel Summer" (2019)

"Anti-Hero" (2022)

Taylor's music and messages to fans create a strong community. This has made her one of the most **streamed** artists worldwide!

GLOSSARY

Billboard—related to a well-known music news magazine and website that ranks songs and albums

charities—organizations that help others in need

CMA Awards—a yearly event during which awards are presented for achievements in country music; CMA stands for Country Music Association.

contract—an agreement between two or more people

food banks—places that give food to people in need

Grammy Awards—yearly awards given by the Recording Academy of the United States for achievements in music; Grammy Awards are also called Grammys.

inspired—gave an idea about what to do or create

natural disasters—sudden events in nature that cause great damage or loss

record label—a company that sells music

relatable—able to be understood and connected to another person's experiences

released—made music available for listening

solo—relating to music performed by one person

streamed—listened to or played online

TO LEARN MORE

AT THE LIBRARY

Anderson, Kirsten. *Who Is Taylor Swift?* New York, N.Y.: Penguin Workshop, 2024.

Burk, Rachelle. *The Story of Taylor Swift: An Inspiring Biography for Young Readers*. Naperville, Ill.: Callisto Publishing, 2024.

Rose, Rachel. *Taylor Swift: Singer, Songwriter, and Activist*. Minneapolis, Minn.: Bearport Publishing, 2023.

ON THE WEB

FACTSURFER

Factsurfer.com gives you a safe, fun way to find more information.

1. Go to www.factsurfer.com.

2. Enter "Taylor Swift" into the search box and click 🔍.

3. Select your book cover to see a list of related content.

INDEX

albums, 10, 12, 14, 16, 17, 18, 19, 20
awards, 12, 13, 15, 18, 21
baking, 16
Big Machine, 11
Billboard, 6, 12, 14, 16, 21
charities, 7
childhood, 8, 9, 10, 11
contract, 10, 11
family, 8, 10
fans, 5, 14, 20, 21
favorites, 9
instruments, 4, 6, 9

playlist, 21
profile, 7
records, 5, 6, 21
sales, 17
songs, 4, 5, 9, 11, 12, 14, 16, 20, 21
Sony Music Publishing, 10
Swifties, 20
Tennessee, 10
timeline, 12–13
tour, 4, 5, 18
types of music, 6, 8, 12, 17

The images in this book are reproduced through the courtesy of: NurPhoto SRL/ Alamy Live News/ Alamy, front cover (Taylor Swift); Catsense, front cover (lights); Noam Galai/ TAS24/ Getty Images, pp. 3, 6, 23; Taya Ovod, pp. 2-3 (background); Shirlaine Forrest/ TAS24/ Getty Images, p. 4; Gareth Cattermole/ TAS24/ Getty Images, p. 5; John Phillips/ Alamy, p. 7; Liam McBurney/ Alamy, p. 7 (infographic); Tammie Arroyo/ Alamy, p. 8; Jason L Nelson/ Alamy, p. 9; HammadKhn, p. 9 (13); grafvision, p. 9 (coffee); Film Fan/ Wikipedia, p. 9 (*Love Actually*); yyuuuyu, p. 9 (cat); Kevin Mazur/ Getty Images, pp. 10, 12-13; Jeff Kravitz/ Getty Images, p. 11; CarlosVdeHabsburgo/ Wikipedia, pp. 12 (Grammy Awards), 15 (Grammy Awards); Dabarti CGI, pp. 12-13 (timeline mixing board); jbrink, pp. 12-13, 21 (playlist); Rick Diamond/ WireImage/ Getty Images, p. 14; WFDJ_Stock, p. 15 (MTV Video Music Awards); s_bukley, p. 15 (CMA Awards, American Music Awards); one-image photography/ Alamy, p. 16; JOHN ANGELILLO/ Alamy, p. 17; John Shearer/ TAS Rights Management/ Getty Images, pp. 18-19; JULIEN DE ROSA/ AFP/ Getty Images, p. 19; Christopher Polk/ TAS/ Getty Images, p. 20; Aldara Zarraoa/ Stringer/ Getty Images, p. 21.